Harar, Ethiopia

Whether or not you would like to become surrounded by individuals or seize a spot exactly where almost nobody goes, shoot incredible artwork and architecture, or simply go to locations of pure magic or drama, we have ten from the very best locations on the planet to go. Consider your choose. Each place on this checklist ensures you extraordinary photos.

Truthfully, this checklist might have 1000's of entries, however the couple of talked about right here possess a track record for carrying out before a digital camera. As soon as you have produced your way via the checklist, make sure to depart a remark together with your preferred location. As lengthy we've billed batteries and open up memory playing cards, we will by no means quit searching for locations to shoot.

If you are searching for a refreshing viewpoint on lifestyle, a wealthy tradition and new sceneries, Harar tops the checklist of most intriguing locations. You will find numerous shrines and mosques, marketplaces along with a charming populace that welcomes new inhabitants. Oh, it is also recognized for the very best high quality espresso.

Harar (Harari:), and recognized to its inhabitants as Gey (Harari:), is really a walled metropolis in japanese Ethiopia. It had been previously the money of Hararghe and now the money from the contemporary Harari Area of Ethiopia. The town is found on the hilltop within the japanese extension from the Ethiopian Highlands, about 5 hundred kilometers from Addis Ababa at an elevation of one,885 meters.

According to figures in the Central Statistical Company in 2005, Harar experienced an approximated complete populace of 122,000, of whom sixty,000 had been males and sixty two,000 had been women. Based on the census of 1994, on which this estimate relies, the town experienced a populace of seventy six,378.

For hundreds of years, Harar continues to be a significant industrial middle, connected from the trade routes using the relaxation of Ethiopia, the whole Horn of Africa, the Arabian Peninsula, and, via its ports, the surface globe. Harar Jugol, the previous walled metropolis, was outlined as being a

Globe Heritage Website in 2006 by UNESCO in recognition of its cultural heritage. It's occasionally recognized in Arabic as "the Metropolis of Saints". Based on UNESCO, it's "considered 'the fourth holy city' of Islam" with one hundred ten mosques, 3 of which day in the tenth century and 102 shrines.

The Fath Madinat Harar information the cleric Abadir Umar ar-Rida and a number of other other spiritual leaders settled in Harar circa 1216 (612 hijri many years). Harar was later on produced the brand new money from the Adal Sultanate in 1520 from the Sultan Abu Bakr ibn Muhammad. The town noticed a political decrease throughout the following Emirate of Harar, only regaining some importance within the Khedivate of

Egypt time period. Throughout the Ethiopian Empire, the town decayed whilst sustaining a particular cultural status. These days, it's the seat from the Harari Area.

Jujuy Province, Argentina

This is actually the northwest of Argentina. Along with a Globe Heritage website, the colourful rock sceneries could make to get a fantastic photograph shoot place. This a part of Argentina is especially well-known for your prosperity of conventional tradition and nationwide elegance.

Pre-Columbian inhabitants referred to as the Omaguacas and Ocloyas, who had been later on conquered from the Incas throughout their growth time period, practiced agriculture and domesticated the guanaco. They'd huts made from mud, and erected stone fortresses to guard their villages. An instance of this kind of fortresses is Pucará de Tilcara, Pucará which means "fortress" (phrase also utilized for the Argentine fight plane Pucara).

In 1593, a little settlement was erected within the Jujuy valley from the work of Francisco de Argañaraz y Murguía. Regardless of the assaults from the Calchaquíes and Omaguacas aborigines, the populace and action from the village consolidated and grew.

At the conclusion of the seventeenth century, the customs towards the Viceroyalty of Peru was transferred from Córdoba to Jujuy.

Using the separation from Peru and also the development from the Viceroyalty from the Río de la Plata, Jujuy misplaced its significance and its populace began to decrease.

Throughout the Might Revolution and also the battles for your independence from the United provinces from the South, numerous confrontations happened in Jujuy since the Spanish concentrated their forces in Peru. The individuals of Jujuy experienced to endure the Jujuy Exodus, an enormous evacuation having a scorched earth coverage, led by Common Manuel Belgrano. Lastly the Spanish surrendered, however the war critically impacted the economic climate from the region.

Following a sequence of inner conflicts, the province declared its autonomy from Tucumán and Salta Provinces on November eighteen, 1834. Jujuy began a gradual technique of financial and social enhancement, and at the conclusion of the nineteenth century, the sugarcane business arose. In the starting from the subsequent century, the railway currently linked the province with Buenos Aires, and La Paz, Bolivia.

Hefty business initial arrived in Jujuy in the hand of Common Manuel Savio, a presidential financial advisor who, in 1945, experienced Argentina's initial contemporary metal mill set up in Jujuy. In 1969, Jujuy joined oil-rich neighboring Salta

Province using the discovery of petroleum from the state-owned YPF.

Tbilisi, Georgia

from the much more underrated journey locations might be Tbilisi. The altering cityscape of Georgia's money offer every thing conceivable for photographers, and it is definitely the aspiration location to get a foodie.

Tbilisi (English: /tb'lisi, t'blsi/ t-bih-LEE-see, t-BIL-ih-see; Georgian: [tbilisi] in a few nations also nonetheless named by its pre-1936 worldwide designation Tiflis (/'tfls/ TIF-liss), will be the money and also the biggest metropolis of Ga, lying around the banking institutions from the Kura River having a populace of roughly one.five million individuals. Started within the fifth century Advertisement by Vakhtang I Gorgasali, the monarch from the Kingdom of Iberia, Tbilisi because served because the money of varied Georgian kingdoms and republics. In between 1801 and 1917, then a part of the Russian Empire, Tbilisi was the seat from the Imperial Viceroy, governing each Southern and Northern Caucasus.

Due to its place around the crossroads in between Europe and Asia, and its proximity towards the profitable Silk Street, all through background Tbilisi was some extent of competition in between numerous international powers. The city's place to at the present time guarantees its place being an essential transit route for numerous power and trade tasks. Tbilisi's various background is mirrored in its architecture, that is a mixture of medieval, neoclassical, Beaux Arts, Artwork Nouveau, Stalinist and Modernstructures.

Traditionally, Tbilisi continues to be house to individuals of numerous cultural, ethnic, and spiritual backgrounds, although it's presently overwhelmingly Japanese Orthodox Christian. Its noteworthy vacationer locations consist of cathedrals Sameba and Sioni, Independence Sq., Rustaveli Avenue and Agmashenebeli Avenue, medieval Narikala Fortress, the pseudo-Moorish Opera Theater, and also the Georgian Nationwide Museum.

Sydney, Australia

In the event you allow it to be so far as Australia, inspiration will strike you whenever you minimum anticipate it. The Opera Home was lately upgraded, and when you are enthusiastic about songs or even the arts, include Sydney for your checklist.

Sydney (/'sdni/) will be the condition money of latest South Wales and also the most populous metropolis in Australia and Oceania Situated on Australia's east coastline, the metropolis surrounds the world's biggest all-natural harbour and sprawls about 70 km (forty three.five mi) on its periphery in the direction of the Blue Mountains towards the west, Hawkesburyto the north and Macarthur towards the south. Sydney is produced up of 658 suburbs, forty nearby authorities locations and fifteen contiguous areas. Citizens from the metropolis are referred to as "Sydneysiders". As of June 2016 Sydney's approximated populace was five,029,768.

The Sydney region continues to be inhabited by indigenous Australians for a minimum of thirty,000 many years. Lieutenant James Cook dinner initial landed at Kurnell in 1770, when navigating his way up the east coastline of Australia on his ship, HMS Endeavour. It had been not till 1788 once the Initial Fleet, which contained convicts and was led by Captain Arthur Phillip, arrived in Botany Bay to discovered Sydney as being a penal colony, the very first European settlement in Australia. Phillip named the town "Sydney" in recognition of

Thomas Townshend, 1st Viscount Sydney, House Secretary in 1788. You will find illustrations of rock artwork and engravings situated in the guarded Ku-ring-gai Chase Nationwide Park, along with the Royal Nationwide Park.

Because convict transportation resulted in the mid-19th century, the town has remodeled from the colonial outpost right into a significant international cultural and financial centre. The municipal council of Sydney was integrated in 1842 and have become Australia's initial metropolis. Gold was found within the colony in 1851 and with it arrived a large number of individuals looking for to create cash. Sydney grew to become among the most multicultural metropolitan areas within the globe following the mass migration subsequent the next Globe War. Based on the 2011 census, much more than 250 various languages had been spoken in Sydney and about forty % of citizens spoke a language apart from English at your home. Moreover, 36 % from the populace noted getting been born abroad.

Regardless of becoming among the most costly metropolitan areas within the globe, the 2014 Mercer High quality of Residing Study ranks Sydney tenth within the globe when it comes to high quality of residing, which makes it among the most livable metropolitan areas. It's categorized being an Alpha Globe Metropolis by Globalization and Globe Metropolitan areas Study Community, indicating its affect within the area and through the entire globe. Rated eleventh within the globe for financial chance, Sydney has a sophisticated marketplace economic climate with strengths in finance, production and tourism. There's a substantial focus of international banking institutions and multinational companies in Sydney and also the metropolis is promoted as certainly one of Asia Pacific's top monetary hubs. Set up in 1850, the College of Sydney is Australia's initial college and it is thought to be among the world's top universities.

Additionally to internet hosting occasions like the 2000 Summer time Olympics, Sydney is among the very best fifteen most-visited metropolitan areas within the globe, with hundreds of thousands of vacationers coming every year to determine the city's landmarks. Its all-natural attributes consist of Sydney Harbour, the Royal Nationwide Park, and also the Royal Botanic Backyard. Man-made points of interest this kind of as Sydney Tower, the Sydney Harbour Bridge, and also the Sydney Opera Home (which grew to become a Globe Heritage Website in 2007), can also be nicely recognized to worldwide guests. The primary passenger airport serving the metropolitan region is Kingsford-Smith Airport, among the world's oldest regularly working airports. Opened in 1906, Central station will be the primary hub from the city's rail network.

Oaxaca, Mexico

Mexico is among probably the most culturally wealthy and various nations. A much less frequented location will be the Mexican condition of Oaxaca. If you are into crafts and textiles, begin preparing your journey to incorporate other metropolitan areas if you wish to discover the nation.

Oaxaca (English: /w'hk/ w-HAH-k, Spanish: [wa'xaka] from Nahuatl languages: Huaxyacac, pronounced [wa'jakak] formally the Totally free and Sovereign Condition of Oaxaca (Spanish: Estado Libre y Soberano de Oaxaca), is among the 31 states which, together with Mexico Metropolis, make up the 32 federative entities of Mexico. It's divided into 570 municipalities, of which 418 (nearly 3 quarters) are ruled from the method of Usos y costumbres (customs and traditions) with acknowledged nearby types of self-governance. Its money metropolis is Oaxaca de Juárez.

Oaxaca is found in Southwestern Mexico. It's bordered from the states of Guerrero towards the west, Puebla towards the northwest, Veracruz towards the north, Chiapas towards the east. Towards the south, Oaxaca features a substantial shoreline around the Pacific Ocean.

The condition is very best recognized for its indigenous peoples and cultures. Probably the most many and very best recognized would be the Zapotecs and also the Mixtecs, but you will find sixteen which are formally acknowledged. These cultures have survived a lot better than most other people in Mexico because of towards the state's rugged and isolating terrain. Most reside in the Central Valleys area, that is also an economically essential region for tourism, with individuals captivated for its archeological websites this kind of as Monte Albán, and Mitla, and its numerous indigenous cultures and crafts. An additional essential vacationer region will be the coastline, that has the main vacation resort of Huatulco and sandy seashores of Puerto Escondido, Puerto Ángel, Zipolite, Bahia de Tembo, and Mazunte. Oaxaca can also be 1 from the most biologically various states in Mexico, rating within the leading 3, together with Chiapas and Veracruz, for figures of reptiles, amphibians, mammals and vegetation.

Vienna, Austria

Relaxation certain this will be the metropolis that's totally obsessive about artwork. For a lot of creatives, Vienna offers all of the benefits. Of course, the meals will maintain you planning to arrive back again.

Vienna (/vi'n/ (German: Wien, pronounced [vin]) will be the money and biggest metropolis of Austria and among the 9 states of Austria. Vienna is Austria's main metropolis, having a populace of about one.eight million (two.six million inside the metropolitan region, almost 1 3rd of Austria's populace), and its cultural, financial, and political centre. It's the 7th-largest metropolis by populace inside metropolis limitations within the European Union. Till the start from the twentieth century, it had been the biggest German-speaking metropolis within the globe, and prior to the splitting from the Austro-Hungarian Empire in Globe War I, the town experienced two million inhabitants. These days, it's the next biggest quantity of German speakers following Berlin. Vienna is host to numerous significant worldwide companies, such as the United Nationsand OPEC. The town is found within the japanese component of Austria and it is near towards the borders from the Czech Republic, Slovakia, and Hungary. These areas function with each other inside a

European Centrope border area. Together with close by Bratislava, Vienna types a metropolitan area with three million inhabitants. In 2001, the town centre was specified a UNESCO Globe Heritage Website. In July 2017 it had been moved towards the checklist of Globe Heritage at risk.

Aside from becoming thought to be the town of Songs due to its musical legacy, Vienna can also be stated to become "The Metropolis of Dreams" simply because it had been house towards the world's initial psychotherapist - Sigmund Freud. The city's roots lie in early Celtic and Roman settlements that remodeled right into a Medieval and Baroque metropolis, and after that the money from the Austro-Hungarian

Empire. It's nicely recognized for getting performed an important function as being a top European songs centre, in the fantastic age of Viennese Classicism with the early component from the twentieth century. The historic centre of Vienna is wealthy in architectural ensembles, such as Baroque castles and gardens, and also the late-19th-century Ringstraße lined with grand structures, monuments and parks.

Vienna is thought for its higher standard of living. Inside a 2005 research of 127 globe metropolitan areas, the Economist Intelligence Device rated the town initial (inside a tie with Vancouver, Canada and San Francisco, United states) for your world's most habitable metropolitan areas. In between 2011 and 2015, Vienna was rated 2nd, powering Melbourne, Australia. For 8 consecutive many years (2009-2016), the human-resource-consulting company Mercer rated Vienna initial in its yearly "Quality of Living" study of a huge selection of metropolitan areas all over the world, a title the town nonetheless held in 2016. Monocle's 2015 "Quality of Lifestyle Survey" rated Vienna 2nd on the checklist from the leading twenty five metropolitan areas within the globe "to create a foundation inside."

The UN-Habitat categorized Vienna because the most affluent metropolis within the globe in 2012/2013. The town was rated 1st globally for its tradition of innovation in 2007 and 2008, and sixth globally (from 256 metropolitan areas) within the 2014

Innovation Metropolitan areas Index, which analyzed 162 indicators in masking 3 locations: tradition, infrastructure, and marketplaces. Vienna frequently hosts city preparing conferences and it is frequently utilized as being a situation research by city planners.

In between 2005 and 2010, Vienna was the world's number-one location for worldwide congresses and conventions. It draws in more than six.eight million vacationers a yr.

North Shore, Oahu, Hawaii

Questioning a couple of much more calm, rural landscape and alter of surroundings The North Shore is legendary for your waves, the farmers and usually a special encounter and way of life.

The northern hemisphere winter season months around the North Shore see a focus of browsing action, benefiting from swells originating within the stormy North Pacific. Noteworthy browsing places consist of Waimea Bay and Sunset Seaside.

The place of Ehukai Seaside, generally recognized because the Banzai Pipeline, will be the most noteworthy browsing place around the North Shore, and it is regarded as a first-rate place for competitions because of to its near proximity towards the seaside, providing spectators, judges, and photographers an excellent see.

The North Shore is taken into account to become the browsing mecca from the globe, and each December hosts 3 competitions, which make up the Triple Crown of Browsing. The 3 men's competitions would be the Reef Hawaiian Professional, the O'Neill Globe Cup of Browsing, and also the Billabong Pipeline Masters. The 3 women's competitions would be the Reef Hawaiian Professional, the Roxy Professional Sunset, and also the Billabong Professional around the neighboring island of Maui.

Waimea Bay performs host towards the Quiksilver Large Wave Invitational in Memory of Eddie Aikau. This really is an unique competitors and individuals should be invited. The competitions features a scheduled window of dates every winter season, nevertheless the competitors features a minimal necessity of 20-foot (six.one m) waves. Consequently, the competitors isn't held each year.

Malmö, Sweden

Sweden is really a distinctive location with nearly one hundred eighty various nationalities. Seems, this is actually the location exactly where all of the foodies visit simply because you are able to probably the most uncommon cuisines. Useless to mention, the surroundings and working day to working day lifestyle is one thing you will wish to doc.

Malmö (IPA: /'mælmo, 'mlmo/; Swedish pronunciation: [²malmø] ; Danish: Malmø) will be the money and biggest metropolis from the Swedish county of Scania. The metropolis is really a gamma globe metropolis (as outlined from the GaWC) and it is the 3rd biggest metropolis in Sweden, following Stockholm and Gothenburg, and also the sixth biggest metropolis in Scandinavia, having a populace of over three hundred,000. The Malmö Metropolitan Area is house to seven hundred,000 individuals, and also the Øresund Area, which incorporates Malmö, is house to three.nine million individuals.

Malmö was 1 from the earliest and many industrialized cities of Scandinavia, however it struggled using the adaptation to postindustrialism. Because the development from the Øresund Bridge, Malmö has gone through a significant transformation with architectural developments, and it's captivated new biotech and IT businesses, and especially college students via Malmö College, started in 1998. The town consists of numerous historic structures and parks, and it is also a industrial centre for your western a part of Scania.

Jordan Trail

For your much more adventurous people, the four hundred mile path is really a climbing route via historical trade routes. There is eight sections, and you will reach see various cityscapes at each stage from the way. A bit of background, along with a entire large amount of photogenic places.

Jordan Path is really a 650 km (four hundred mi) lengthy path in Jordan. Set up in 2015 from the Jordan Path Affiliation, which aims to revive Jordan's tourism sector following getting confronted setbacks in early 2010s.

The path stretches from Umm Qais in northern Jordan towards the coastal metropolis of Aqaba in its south. The path passes via fifty two villages and cities, however the path continues to be dissected to 35 sections. The whole size from the path requires about forty times to finish.

The path obtained in depth media protection following its inception, and it has been named as amongst 2018's very best vacationer locations within the globe to go to by Nationwide Geographic, the British Sunday Occasions, the Guardian, Condenast, Vogue US and Lonely Earth.

Dublin, Ireland

Frequently known as "Europe's biggest village", Dublin is really a really energetic metropolis having a fantastic vibe. Historic websites, pubs, museums and galleries, also as unforgettable landscapes and character throughout you.

Dublin (/'dbln/, Irish: Baile Átha Cliath Irish pronunciation: [bl 'cli]) will be the money of and biggest metropolis in Eire. Dublin is found within the province of Leinster around the east coastline of eire, in the mouth from the River Liffey and bordered around the South from the Wicklow Mountains. The town has an city region populace of one,173,179. The populace from the Dublin Area, as of 2016, was one,347,359 individuals, and also the populace from the Higher Dublin region was one,904,806.

There's archaeological discussion concerning exactly exactly where Dublin was set up by Celtic-speaking individuals within the seventh century. Later on expanded as being a Viking settlement, the dominion of Dublin grew to become Ireland's principal metropolis subsequent the Norman invasion. The town expanded quickly in the seventeenth century and was briefly the next biggest metropolis within the British Empire prior to the Functions of Union in 1800. Subsequent the partition of eire in 1922, Dublin grew to become the money from the Irish Totally free Condition, later on renamed Eire.

As of 2010, Dublin was outlined from the Globalization and Globe Metropolitan areas Study Community (GaWC) as being a international metropolis, having a rating of "Alpha-", which locations it among the very best 30 metropolitan areas on the planet. It's a historic and modern centre for training, the humanities, administration, economic climate and business.

www.ingramcontent.com/pod-product-compliance
Lightning Source LLC
Chambersburg PA
CBHW030103230526
45471CB00003B/1239